HOT
CHOCOLATE

50 HEAVENLY CUPS OF COMFORT

FRED THOMPSON

THE HARVARD COMMON PRESS
BOSTON, MASSACHUSETTS

The Harvard Common Press
535 Albany Street
Boston, Massachusetts 02118
www.harvardcommonpress.com

Printed in China
Printed on acid-free paper

Library of Congress Cataloging-in-Publication Data

Thompson, Fred, 1953-
  Hot Chocolate : 50 heavenly cups of comfort / Fred Thompson.
     p. cm.
  Includes index.
  ISBN 1-55832-290-6 (hardcover : alk. paper)
  1. Chocolate drinks. I. Title.
  TX817.C4T56 2006
  641.8'75—dc22

                                        2006002865

ISBN-13: 978-1-55832-290-5
ISBN-10: 1-55832-290-6

Special bulk-order discounts are available on this and other Harvard Common Press books.
Companies and organizations may purchase books for premiums or resale, or may arrange a
custom edition, by contacting the Marketing Director at the address above.

Book design by Elizabeth Van Itallie
Photographs by Brian Hagiwara
Food styling by Fred Thompson

10 9 8 7 6 5 4 3

In memory of Al Haskins, Jr.,
who consumed chocolate almost every day
of his 92 years

Contents

Acknowledgments

Being in the right place, at the right time, with the right folks, sure can pay off. While at a conference in the Napa Valley, Suzanne Hamlin and Janet Fletcher, both well-known food writers, complimented me on my cookbooks *Iced Tea* and *Lemonade* and wondered what I was going to do next. While I stumbled for an answer, they simultaneously suggested that I write one on hot chocolate. Thus a book was born. Now my "liquid" trilogy is complete.

The staff at Scharffen Berger Chocolates in Berkeley, California, who showed me how chocolate is made and fielded a bunch of questions, deserve a thank-you. They made writing this book a joy.

A big thanks to Bruce Shaw and his great staff at The Harvard Common Press: executive editor Valerie Cimino, creative services manager Virginia Downes, managing editor Christine Corcoran Cox, project manager Patricia Jalbert-Levine, production editor Abby Collier, associate publisher Christine Alaimo, sales director Betsy Young, publicity manager Liza Beth, special sales associate Megan Weireter, marketing assistant Amy Etcheson, and office manager Ellie Levine. Thanks also go to Jayne Yaffe Kemp, a super copyeditor.

Brian Hagiwara, as usual, makes the photographs jump from the page. They will make you want to run and try one of my hot chocolates. His talents are much appreciated. Nikki Parrish was there with all manner of word-processing help and was always willing to test a recipe. My neighbors the Johnsons and the Thomases drank many a cup of hot chocolate, both good and bad. And Belinda Ellis, who was full of ideas, taught me how to make marshmallows. You'll meet other people in the pages of this book who shared ideas and recipes with me.

I've had much help and encouragement in my writing career. Folks like Susan Houston, my editor at the Raleigh *News & Observer;* Toni Allegra and Don Fry from the Greenbrier Symposium for Professional Food Writers; and Pam Hoenig all have had an impact on the way I view food and writing.

A special thanks to Laura, who has always thought it was cool that her dad writes cookbooks.

Introduction

Hot chocolate is winter's gift to our soul. Nothing completes a roaring fire better than a cup of hot chocolate and someone to snuggle with. And more and more, hot chocolate is becoming the beverage of choice for a morning eye-opener, a midmorning pick-me-up, or an afternoon stress reliever. No longer is this elixir just the domain of children—it truly has taken its place in the adult world.

My earliest memory of hot chocolate was the cup that my dad would buy for me at ice hockey games when I was in middle school. I thought I was pretty cocky walking around with a hot beverage. It seemed so grown-up at the time, and it started a love affair with hot chocolate that has lasted for many years. Of course, that concession-stand hot chocolate was pumped out of a machine and looked more antique white than coffee with cream. Back then, almost all "hot chocolate" was really hot cocoa. In those days that's all I knew: a little chocolate flavor with a lot of hot milk.

Fast-forward to a few years ago, when I had my first taste of a European-style hot chocolate made with bar chocolate, not cocoa powder. The taste was revolutionary: serious chocolate flavor with just a touch of milk or cream. That cup launched a worldwide search for hot chocolate. Trips across the country, south of the border, and to Italy and France, along with the cultural mix in New York City, where I live, have introduced me to some extraordinary ways with hot chocolate. I'd like to share the best of those with you.

THE BASICS

A Quick History of Hot Chocolate

Chocolate has been drunk for thousands of years, most archaeologists agree, but it was the Mayans who really got the ball rolling by developing savory chocolate drinks. They also used cocoa beans as currency. In the 1500s the Aztecs introduced a little sweetness to the mixture in the form of honey. The explorer Hernando Cortés brought chocolate back to Spain from his explorations in the New World. He also learned from the Mexican emperor Montezuma that chocolate has aphrodisiac properties. The Spaniards blended sugar with their hot chocolate, and it soon became the drink of the rich elite. And if you think the coffeehouse craze is a new concept, you may be surprised to learn that London had "chocolate houses" in the 1700s, and they were quite the rage. Writers, politicos, and socialites alike would gather at these spots to hash out the events of the day. The English have the distinction of being the first to blend milk into chocolate, at the beginning of the 1700s.

In 1764, in what is now the city of Dorchester, Massachusetts, the first American chocolate manufacturer opened its doors. The company was called, as it is today, Baker's Chocolate. As the Industrial Revolution continued, the Dutch developed a chocolate press, and that, coupled with a drop in sugar prices, allowed the masses to enjoy chocolate. The Europeans continued their stronghold on chocolate making until the early twentieth century, when a successful caramel maker, Milton Hershey, decided that chocolate was the future. "Caramels are a fad, but chocolate is a permanent thing," he is believed to have said. Well, caramel wasn't a fad, but he was right about chocolate—it is a permanent part of the world's culture. While Hershey has been the dominant chocolate maker in the United States, other, smaller companies are quickly expanding America's taste for more upscale and cacao-loaded pleasures.

Thomas Jefferson predicted that chocolate would overtake tea and coffee as the most popular drink in America. He might have been off on the drinking part, but chocolate in one form or another has become a staple of our everyday life.

Today, chocolate styles vary greatly from country to country. French and Belgian chocolate makers look down their noses at the British and Americans for the inclusion of milk in chocolate bars. They prefer the flavors of bittersweet or semisweet or even unsweetened chocolate to the milk chocolate that so many of us have grown up with in America. But our exposure is changing. More and more, high-quality chocolates are being imported into the United States, and chocolate makers and bakers alike continue to introduce us to new flavor concepts. We also are very fortunate in this country to have a chocolate maker like Scharffen Berger in Berkeley, California, which has brought high-end, exceptionally delicious European-style chocolate to our shores.

Most of our exposure in this country to hot chocolate has been through a combination of cocoa powder and milk. Not bad, but not great. In exploring the world of hot chocolate, I found that true chocolate, what you find in chocolate bars or even chocolate chips, makes a much better centerpiece for hot chocolate than cocoa powder does. But then, not all varieties of chocolate are created equal. So just what the heck is chocolate?

Chocolate's Origins and Types

Theobroma cacao, literally the "food of the gods" in Latin, is not a bad name for chocolate. The cacao tree, the source of all chocolate, is a tropical plant bearing fruit with pods that are as big as 12 inches long. Almost all chocolate is harvested within 20 degrees of the equator, north or south. This region is called the cacao belt. It takes the cacao tree about five years to start producing bean-bearing pods, but it will produce pods for anywhere from 20 to 50 years. The cacao beans are harvested and then cleaned and roasted much like coffee to bring out their full flavor and aroma. The outer shells are removed, leaving the cacao nibs, the edible part of the bean. The nibs then go into a machine called the "mélange," which crushes and exposes the fat, adding enough heat and force to turn the nibs into chocolate liquor. Chocolate liquor is the base material for all chocolate products. From this point, different manufacturers complete the process of making chocolate in different ways, but they all employ certain standards.

- **BITTER (OR UNSWEETENED) CHOCOLATE,** which most of us know as baking or cooking chocolate, is basically chocolate liquor that has been cooled and molded, with no added sugar. Most bitter chocolate will be 99 percent cacao. The percentage is an indication of the chocolate content in the bar.

- **BITTERSWEET OR DARK CHOCOLATE** contains a little sugar but still maintains a strong chocolate presence. Most good bittersweets will range from 65 percent to 70 percent or more cacao.

- **SEMISWEET CHOCOLATE,** which is most common to all of us, is produced by adding more cocoa butter and sugar back into the chocolate liquor. It's thoroughly mixed, and then the chocolate is molded into bars or chips. Semisweet chocolate can be as low as 35 percent cacao.

- **SWEET DARK CHOCOLATE** is simply a combination of bitter chocolate, sugar, and cocoa butter, with the addition of vanilla.

- **MILK CHOCOLATE** is a favorite choice for candy bars and eating chocolates. Milk chocolate is a combination of chocolate liqueur, additional cocoa butter, sugar, milk or cream, and a little vanilla. Again, it's thoroughly mixed and processed into bars and chips.

- **COCOA POWDER** is the portion of the chocolate that remains after most of the cocoa butter has been removed. Dutch-processed cocoa powder has been treated with an alkali to neutralize cocoa's acidity. It is darker and richer than regular, or natural, cocoa powder. There is also another type of cocoa powder sometimes referred to as "breakfast cocoa," which contains at least 22 percent cocoa butter, making it a high-fat and very rich cocoa powder.

- **DRINKING CHOCOLATE** is a new addition to the chocolate market. Most manufacturers use a mix of cocoa powder and ground chocolate in some form.

Yes, Hot Chocolate Really Is Good for You

"Chocolate" has become a health buzzword of late. Studies suggest that the chemical makeup of chocolate improves mood. But the latest research on chocolate focuses on the antioxidants present in its chemical base. Antioxidants seem to protect against heart disease, especially fighting LDLs, or "bad" cholesterol, and some cancers. Pure cocoa powder has the most antioxidants, followed by baking and dark chocolate, then milk chocolate. Milk chocolate has the same amount of antioxidants as a five-ounce glass of red wine. Most medical researchers agree that the darker the chocolate (with higher percentages of cacao), the greater the health benefit. Fortunately, there are more dark chocolates available at the retail level than ever before. Of course, this news come with a caveat—chocolate is still high in fat and sugar. But at least now when you indulge in chocolate's guilty pleasure, you know you are getting more than just calories.

How to Make Fabulous Hot Chocolate

So when the hot chocolate is rich and creamy, who cares about calories? Just mellow into a sensual taste experience. Hot chocolate is easy to make and requires no special equipment. Just a chocolate bar, water, heat, and a mug will give you terrific hot chocolate. Some tools and tricks will make life a bit easier, though. A good chef's knife to chop chocolate bars is great. Those specialty chocolate-chipping tools aren't necessary. Always chop chocolate from a point on the edge of the bar, rotating the bar around to keep the point. Try to shave the chocolate, which will allow it to melt faster and smoother, with less chance of scorching. Use a double boiler until you become confident enough to melt chocolate over direct heat. A good balloon whisk and some wooden spoons are also helpful. If you really get into making hot chocolate, you might want to dazzle your friends with a *molinillo* (moh-lee-NEE-oh), the Mexican wooden whisk-type tool used to froth or foam hot chocolate.

Most of us think of hot chocolate as containing milk, but blending chocolate with water will actually give you the most intense chocolate flavor. Low-fat and fat-free milks are good choices if you want just a bit of creaminess. Chocolate flavor lessens in intensity as you increase the fat content with whole milk, half-and-half, and heavy cream. All options are delicious, and all have their place, depending on the recipe and your mood, or what's in your refrigerator when the urge for hot chocolate strikes.

What brand of chocolate should you use? Should it be imported or domestic? How about a high-end versus a grocery-store variety? This all depends on your tastes and pocketbook. Many of my hot chocolate taste testers found the darker chocolates to be stronger than what they were used to. Other tasters, after sampling a hot chocolate made with 70 percent cacao chocolate, found other hot chocolates bland by comparison. The different chocolates are generally interchangeable in all the recipes in this book, according to your taste, and another way to adjust flavor is with the liquid you use. I used all types of chocolate in developing these recipes. If intense chocolate flavor is your goal, I recommend the higher-end 70 percent cacao chocolates. If you're combining chocolate with other flavors, like peppermint or cinnamon or brandy, less expensive chocolate is perfectly okay. (Mexican chocolate, which is sweeter than other chocolates and has added cinnamon, has no substitute and so is the exception.) Here are a few great varieties to look for, though the list is by no means comprehensive:

Valrhona and Michel Cluizel, France; Callebaut and Nirvana, Belgium; Schokinag, Germany; Max Brenner, Israel; Scharffen Berger, Moonstruck, Vosges, and MarieBelle, United States; and El Rey, Venezuela.

Many of these brands are now in large grocery stores. Places like Whole Foods Market carry a good variety, as do most gourmet and specialty food shops, baking supply stores, and catalogs. Also, good kitchen shops such as Williams-Sonoma and Sur La Table carry a range of these chocolates.

All of these manufacturers also make excellent, and often expensive, cocoa powder. A good-quality unsweetened grocery store variety works just fine for most recipes.

When making hot chocolate from scratch, don't limit yourself to just these recipes. After you've prepared a few of the hot chocolates and gotten the hang of hot chocolate making, experiment and have some fun with what you think could be a great hot chocolate. That's what time in the kitchen should be about—creativity and fun. To kick things off, here are three recipes for fabulous garnishes for any of the hot chocolate drinks that follow.

Vanilla Marshmallows

These marshmallows are awesome. Give them a try at least once. They are not that labor-intensive, and the flavor is well worth the extra trouble.

Three ¼-ounce envelopes unflavored gelatin
½ cup cold water
2½ cups sugar
¾ cup light corn syrup
½ cup hot water
¼ teaspoon salt
2 teaspoons pure vanilla extract
Confectioners' sugar

1. Cover the inside of a 13 x 9-inch pan with aluminum foil or parchment paper. Coat with nonstick cooking spray.

2. In a large heatproof mixing bowl, combine the gelatin and cold water and stir to mix.

3. Heat the sugar, corn syrup, hot water, and salt in a heavy saucepan over medium-high heat, stirring until the mixture boils. Stop stirring and heat to 240°F, using a candy thermometer.

4. Pour the mixture into the gelatin. Using an electric mixer, whip until the mixture has doubled in size. Fold in the vanilla extract.

5. Spread the mixture evenly into the prepared pan. Allow to cool and set, uncovered, overnight.

6. Using a serrated knife dipped in warm water, cut marshmallows to whatever size you prefer. Toss to coat with confectioners' sugar. Store at room temperature in an airtight container for up to 2 weeks.

MAKES ABOUT 2 DOZEN

Fluffy Egg White Marshmallows

These marshmallows bear a close resemblance to the fluffiness of store-bought marshmallows, but they have a lot more flavor.

Three $\frac{1}{4}$-ounce envelopes unflavored gelatin
$\frac{1}{2}$ cup cold water
$2\frac{1}{2}$ cups sugar
$\frac{2}{3}$ cup light corn syrup
$\frac{1}{2}$ cup hot water
$\frac{1}{4}$ teaspoon salt
2 large egg whites
2 teaspoons pure vanilla extract
Confectioners' sugar

1. Cover the inside of a 13 x 9-inch pan with aluminum foil or parchment paper. Coat with nonstick cooking spray.

2. In a large heatproof mixing bowl, combine the gelatin and cold water and stir to mix.

3. Heat 2 cups of the sugar, the corn syrup, hot water, and salt in a heavy saucepan over medium-high heat, stirring until the mixture boils. Stop stirring and heat to 240°F, using a candy thermometer.

4. Pour the mixture into the gelatin. Using an electric mixer, whip until the mixture has doubled in size.

5. In a large mixing bowl, whip the egg whites with the remaining $\frac{1}{2}$ cup sugar. Slowly pour the gelatin mixture into the egg whites in a steady stream. Fold in the vanilla extract.

6. Spread the mixture evenly into the prepared pan. Allow to cool and set, uncovered, overnight.

7. Using a serrated knife dipped in warm water, cut marshmallows to whatever size you prefer. Toss to coat with confectioners' sugar. Store at room temperature in an airtight container for up to 2 weeks.

MAKES ABOUT 2 DOZEN

Perfect Sweetened Whipped Cream

This whipped cream is perfect for any of the recipes in this book. It is best when used within an hour or so of your making it, and it must be stored, covered, in the refrigerator. You'll want to whip the cream into soft peaks, which means that when you remove the beaters, a peak will form and quickly collapse. If you go a bit beyond this stage, don't worry—it will still taste great.

> **1 cup heavy cream**
> **1 teaspoon pure vanilla extract**
> **1½ tablespoons light corn syrup**

In a medium-size mixing bowl, combine the cream and vanilla extract. Stir in the corn syrup a little at the time. Using an electric mixer, whip until the mixture reaches the soft peak stage.

MAKES 2 CUPS

CLASSIC
HOT
CHOCOLATE

What is classic hot chocolate? It depends on where you live and what your cultural background is, or just how crazy about chocolate you are. Europeans and those in the cacao belt in the Southern Hemisphere have long believed that you melt solid chocolate, add a small amount of liquid, and drink up. Americans are just beginning to learn of the joys of rich, flavorful chocolate, creamy and hot. These recipes will take you around the hot chocolate–loving world, to your taste buds' delight.

Chocolat Chaud • Chocolat Chaud au Mascarpone • American Hot Chocolate with Chocolate Whipped Cream • Italian Hot Chocolate with Orange Whipped Cream • Ecuadorian Heirloom Hot Chocolate • Ancient Aztec Cacahuatl • Austrian Hot Chocolate • Rich Gourmet Hot Chocolate • "Nun's Revenge" Fabulous Italian Hot Chocolate • Vanilla Hot Chocolate • Serious Hot Chocolate

Chocolat Chaud

Within the chocolate-loving regions of Europe, like France, Switzerland, and Belgium, the hot chocolate might surprise you. The chocolate is melted in water and whisked to form a drink that is true chocolate, unadorned with anything else. This recipe is similar to the one from Les Deux Magots, a famous French bistro on Paris's Left Bank. Hemingway and Fitzgerald were among the regulars in their day. The restaurant serves *chocolat chaud* with a sugar cube on the side. Other bistros and cafés may include some warmed milk. This recipe is about as pure a chocolate experience as you will get.

½ cup water
2 ounces bittersweet chocolate, chopped
1 teaspoon sugar (optional)
Warmed milk (optional)

1. Pour the water into a medium-size saucepan and place over medium heat. As soon as the water warms, add the chocolate and begin whisking until the chocolate is smooth and completely melted.

2. Pour the hot chocolate into a mug and serve immediately with the sugar and warmed milk on the side, if desired.

SERVES 1

Chocolat Chaud au Mascarpone

The Angelina Café in Paris makes a delicious twist on traditional hot chocolate. Instead of whipped cream or a marshmallow, a dollop of mascarpone cheese completes each cup (they use demitasse cups). It's a heavenly finish.

6 ounces semisweet or bittersweet chocolate, chopped
¼ cup water
3 cups whole milk
6 tablespoons mascarpone cheese
Sugar to taste

1. In a double boiler over low heat, combine the chocolate and water. Raise the heat to medium and whisk until the chocolate is melted and the mixture is smooth. Divide equally among 6 mugs.

2. Warm the milk in a microwave or in a saucepan over low heat. Pour ½ cup warmed milk into each mug and stir to blend. Add a tablespoon of mascarpone cheese to each mug, and pass the sugar to taste.

SERVES 6

American Hot Chocolate with Chocolate Whipped Cream

U p until the past few years, most Americans have preferred a sweeter hot chocolate than is served in Europe and South America. This hot chocolate incorporates a little more sweetness and creaminess while holding on to a bit of European character. Notice that I've suggested Scharffen Berger products, made in Berkeley, California. They make superb chocolate that rivals the great manufacturers of Europe.

½ cup heavy cream
4 tablespoons plus 1 teaspoon Scharffen Berger cocoa powder
4 tablespoons plus ½ teaspoon sugar
2½ ounces Scharffen Berger bittersweet chocolate
    (70 to 75 percent cacao), chopped
Large pinch of kosher salt
5 cups whole milk
Grated bittersweet chocolate for garnish (optional)

1. In a small bowl using an electric mixer, whip the cream with 1 teaspoon of the cocoa powder and ½ teaspoon of the sugar until it forms firm peaks. Set aside.

2. In a medium-size saucepan, combine the chocolate, the remaining 4 tablespoons cocoa powder and 4 tablespoons sugar, the salt, and the milk. Place the mixture over medium heat; whisk gently. Once the chocolate melts and the cocoa dissolves, raise the heat to medium-high; whisk more vigorously to form a froth on the surface. When the mixture bubbles around the edges and seems ready to boil, remove from the heat. Do not let it boil.

3. Ladle the hot chocolate into 4 cups with some froth on each. Spoon a dollop of chocolate whipped cream on top, and sprinkle with grated chocolate if desired.

SERVES 4

The city of Florence and the Umbria region have some of the most delicious hot chocolates in the world. Don't be fooled by the institutional-looking machines that dispense it.

Italian Hot Chocolate with Orange Whipped Cream

The Italians have some of the most decadent ways with hot chocolate. They also love to combine orange flavor with any type of chocolate, a delicious match.

8 ounces bittersweet chocolate, chopped
2 tablespoons sugar
3 cups whole milk
Zest from 1 orange
1 cup whipped cream for garnish

1. In a double boiler over low heat, warm the chocolate and sugar until melted. Turn off the heat. Slowly whisk in the milk until fully combined.

2. Lightly fold the orange zest into the whipped cream. Pour the hot chocolate into 4 mugs and top each with a dollop of orange whipped cream. Serve immediately.

SERVES 4

Ecuadorian Heirloom Hot Chocolate

C acao beans are like wine grapes: they pick up flavors from the land. In South America, organizations such as the Conservación y Desarrollo partner with the Rainforest Alliance to help produce sustainable plants for cocoa. South American hot chocolate is thinner in style than European hot chocolate, more similar to coffee. Use a good South American chocolate (check the label for the country of origin) to fully capture the floral flavors.

2 ounces bittersweet chocolate (at least 70 percent cacao), chopped
2 tablespoons water
½ cup heavy cream
2 teaspoons sugar
Marshmallow or sweetened whipped cream for garnish (optional)

1. In a double boiler over low heat, combine the chocolate and water. Raise the heat to medium and whisk until the chocolate melts and the mixture is smooth.

2. Warm the cream in a microwave or in a saucepan over low heat. Transfer the chocolate mixture to a food processor or blender, add the sugar, turn on the machine, and slowly add the warm cream.

3. Stop the machine and scrape down the sides. Pour the mixture into a cup. Serve immediately, with a marshmallow or whipped cream if desired.

SERVES 1

The emperor Montezuma reportedly drank nothing but liquid chocolate, downing 50 cups a day from a golden goblet. He thought it to be an aphrodisiac that gave him the stamina to serve his harem, which some believe comprised approximately 600 women.

Ancient Aztec Cacahuatl

This Southern Hemisphere concoction is a bit more sophisticated than many "south of the border" hot chocolates. Infusing the half-and-half with a vanilla bean adds volumes to the finished flavor. Using a pure single chile powder creates more complexity than heat. This one is worth the effort.

5 cups half-and-half
1 vanilla bean, cut in half lengthwise
8 ounces Mexican chocolate, such as Abuelita, chopped
¼ cup natural cocoa powder
1 to 2 teaspoons ancho chile powder, to your taste
3 tablespoons honey
Whipped cream for garnish
1 to 2 tablespoons slivered unsalted roasted almonds for garnish

1. In a medium-size saucepan over medium heat, combine the half-and-half and vanilla bean. Heat until the mixture comes to a simmer.

2 Reduce the heat to low and add the chocolate and cocoa powder. Whisk to combine. Simmer for 5 to 10 minutes, or until the mixture coats the back of a spoon. Watch it closely so that it does not boil over.

3. Add the chile powder, a little at a time, to taste. Stir in the honey and blend. Discard the vanilla bean.

4. Pour the hot chocolate into 8 small cups and top with the whipped cream and slivered almonds.

SERVES 8

Austrian Hot Chocolate

From the Alps comes a hot chocolate that is rich and warm, without cloying sweetness. This type of hot chocolate is really a cross between the Swiss and Austrian versions. Besides having great chocolate, the Alpine countries have sturdy milk, with a tangy flavor. To get an experience closer to the real thing, use a local dairy's milk—the type of dairy that still uses glass jars and processes its milk in a modern, yet artisan, way.

2 ounces bittersweet chocolate (at least 70 percent cacao), chopped
¼ cup water
2 teaspoons sugar
½ cup whole milk
Marshmallow or sweetened whipped cream for garnish (optional)

1. In a double boiler over low heat, combine the chocolate and water. Raise the heat to medium and whisk until the chocolate melts and the mixture is smooth. Add the sugar, whisking to dissolve.

2. Warm the milk in a microwave or in a saucepan over low heat. Slowly pour the warm milk into the chocolate mixture, whisking constantly until smooth and well combined. Pour the mixture into a mug. Serve topped with a marshmallow or whipped cream, if desired.

SERVES 1

Rich Gourmet Hot Chocolate

Here is another gourmet American-style hot chocolate that is quick and simple. Although it's not fancy, use the best ingredients you can find. If you have a local dairy that makes superior heavy cream, spring for it in this recipe.

2 ounces bittersweet chocolate (at least 70 percent cacao), chopped
2 tablespoons water
2 teaspoons sugar
½ cup heavy cream
Marshmallow or sweetened whipped cream for garnish (optional)

1. In a double boiler over low heat, combine the chocolate and water. Raise the heat to medium and whisk until the chocolate melts and the mixture is smooth. Add the sugar and whisk to dissolve.

2. Warm the cream in a microwave or in a saucepan over low heat. Slowly whisk the warm cream into the chocolate mixture and continue whisking until smooth and creamy.

3. Pour the hot chocolate into a cup and top with a marshmallow or whipped cream, if desired.

SERVES 1

John Scharffenberger was an award-winning winemaker in California's Alexander Valley before turning his attention to chocolate in 1997.

"Nun's Revenge" Fabulous Italian Hot Chocolate

A life of piety and chastity has to call for something sensual occasionally. Yes, you can enjoy the seductive chocolate flavor and thick creaminess of this Italian hot chocolate without fearing the loss of other worldly pleasures, but this confection is sure to elicit a moan from all who partake. Drinking any of the great Italian-style hot chocolates is almost a religious experience. Over and over again, people who taste this drink for the first time say, "Oh, my God." Is that enough encouragement to give this one a try? Don't overlook the importance of the orange zest or the arrowroot. The oil from the zest gives the chocolate a fresh kick, and the arrowroot thickens the mixture.

½ cup plus 2 tablespoons half-and-half
1 teaspoon arrowroot
1 tablespoon sugar
2 ounces bittersweet chocolate (at least 70 percent cacao), chopped
2 to 4 strips orange zest for garnish

1. In a small bowl, combine 2 tablespoons of the half-and-half with the arrowroot, whisking until smooth.

2. Place the remaining ½ cup of half-and-half in a small saucepan over medium heat. Bring to a simmer. When the half-and-half begins to bubble around the edges, whisk in the sugar. Whisk in the arrowroot mixture until the half-and-half thickens slightly, usually less than a minute.

3. Remove from the heat and quickly whisk in the chocolate until smooth.

4. Pour into cups, top each with a piece of orange zest, and serve immediately.

SERVES 2 IN CAPPUCCINO CUPS OR 4 IN ESPRESSO CUPS

Hot chocolate has become such a stylish and complex drink that the Ritz-Carlton hotel in Philadelphia has a hot chocolate sommelier on staff to guide customers through its hot chocolate menu.

Vanilla Hot Chocolate

We can't neglect the white chocolate crowd. I like white chocolate, even though it's not "real" chocolate. White chocolate is more or less vanilla-flavored cocoa butter—it contains no chocolate liquor. Make sure you are buying true white chocolate, which will list cocoa butter in the ingredients, rather than confectionery coating. This rich concoction is heavily scented with vanilla. Be sure to garnish it with a little cocoa powder or grated dark chocolate for an extra kick.

1½ cups milk or half-and-half
½ cup vanilla syrup
⅛ teaspoon kosher salt
1 vanilla bean
6 ounces white chocolate, chopped
Marshmallows for garnish
Natural cocoa powder or grated bittersweet chocolate for garnish

1. Pour the milk, vanilla syrup, and salt into a medium-size saucepan. Place over medium heat and cook, stirring until the mixture is hot. Do not let the mixture boil.

2. Split the vanilla bean lengthwise with a small sharp knife and scrape the seeds into the saucepan.

3. Stir in the white chocolate until it has melted and the mixture is smooth. Don't rush this step by turning up the heat—white chocolate has a tendency to seize when heated at too high a temperature.

4. Ladle the hot chocolate into 4 mugs. Top with marshmallows and garnish with a sprinkle of cocoa powder or grated chocolate. Serve immediately.

SERVES 4

Serious Hot Chocolate

So now let's take three different kinds of chocolate, plus cocoa powder, and combine them all into one over-the-top hot chocolate. You will be pleasantly surprised at how nicely this recipe comes together, and the taste—it's something special.

1½ teaspoons sweetened cocoa powder or drinking chocolate
1½ teaspoons Dutch-processed cocoa powder
1½ tablespoons sugar
1 tablespoon salted butter, at room temperature
½ cup whole milk
2 ounces bittersweet chocolate, chopped
2 ounces semisweet chocolate, chopped
2 ounces milk chocolate, chopped
Sweetened whipped cream for garnish
Grated chocolate for garnish

1. Place a double boiler over medium heat. Add the 2 cocoa powders and the sugar. Whisk until the sugar is melted and combined with the cocoa. Beat in the butter, creaming with the sugar.

2. Add a little of the milk. Add the 3 chopped chocolates, whisking as they melt. Slowly add the remaining milk. Whisk until the mixture is smooth, creamy, and hot.

3. Pour into 2 or 3 mugs and serve topped with whipped cream and grated chocolate.

SERVES 2 TO 3

HOT
CHOCOLATE
MIXES
AND SUPER MIXES

There is a long-standing tradition of folks whipping up a batch of hot chocolate mix as the air begins to chill in the fall. Whether it stays around the house or makes it to the office, having a simple and easy-to-prepare hot chocolate mix is a great thing. The problem with so many store-bought mixes is that they are not nearly as dense, rich, or full of flavor as homemade mixes. Those on the following pages are a snap to put together, and they run the full flavor gamut. At the end of this chapter you'll find some mixes with the most intense mouth feel and chocolate flavor. Try some or all of them to find a mix that suits you best. When stored in a cool place in an airtight container, these mixes will last six months, although I bet they'll be consumed long before then.

Classic Hot Cocoa and Chocolate Mix • Cinnamon Chip Hot Chocolate Mix • Peanut Butter Hot Chocolate Mix • Old-Fashioned Peppermint Stick Hot Chocolate Mix • Mocha Hot Chocolate Mix • Mexican Hot Cocoa and Chocolate Mix • Vanilla Hot Chocolate Mix • Super Classic Hot Cocoa and Chocolate Mix • Super Mocha Hot Chocolate Mix • Super Mexican Hot Cocoa and Chocolate Mix

Classic Hot Cocoa and Chocolate Mix

Any cocoa-based hot chocolate mix is classic. I bet you have one in your recipe files. Surprise your family or coworkers with this mix, which has the additional chocolate power of semisweet chips. You will be a real sweet hero.

1 cup sugar
1 cup natural cocoa powder
1 cup nonfat dry powdered milk
½ cup miniature semisweet chocolate chips
2 teaspoons kosher salt
Miniature marshmallows for garnish

1. Combine the sugar, cocoa powder, powdered milk, chocolate chips, and salt in a large bowl. Pour into a 1-quart airtight container. Place the marshmallows in a separate airtight container.

2. For a single serving, scoop ⅓ cup of the mix into a mug and pour 1 cup boiling water over it. Stir until the chocolate chips have melted and the mixture is smooth. Top with marshmallows and serve immediately.

MAKES 1 QUART OF MIX TO YIELD 12 SERVINGS

If you want to make a friend for life, give a gift of homemade hot chocolate mix. Simply layer the components of any of the mixes in this chapter into a large glass jar tied with a colorful ribbon. On the card, tell the recipients to mix thoroughly before using and give them directions on how to prepare single servings.

Cinnamon Chip Hot Chocolate Mix

Here is a twist on the classic hot chocolate mix with a touch of cinnamon. If you prefer a more subtle cinnamon flavor, use ¼ cup each of cinnamon chips and semisweet chocolate chips. You can also substitute cappuccino chips, if you run across them, in this recipe.

1 cup granulated sugar
1 cup natural cocoa powder
1 cup nonfat dry powdered milk
½ cup cinnamon-flavored chips
2 teaspoons kosher salt
Confectioners' sugar for serving

1. Combine the granulated sugar, cocoa powder, powdered milk, cinnamon-flavored chips, and salt in a large bowl. Pour into a 1-quart airtight container.

2. For a single serving, scoop ⅓ cup of the mix into a mug and pour 1 cup boiling water over it. Stir until the cinnamon chips have melted and the mixture is smooth. Dust each serving with confectioners' sugar and serve immediately.

MAKES 1 QUART OF MIX TO YIELD 12 SERVINGS

Peanut Butter Hot Chocolate Mix

This recipe is like a peanut butter cup in a mug. Reese's Peanut Butter Cups are one of this country's best-selling sweet treats, so why not turn its two great tastes—chocolate and peanut butter—into one great hot chocolate?

1 cup sugar
1 cup natural cocoa powder
1 cup nonfat dry powdered milk
½ cup peanut butter chips
1 teaspoon kosher salt

1. Combine the sugar, cocoa powder, powdered milk, peanut butter chips, and salt in a large bowl. Pour into a 1-quart airtight container.

2. For a single serving, scoop ⅓ cup of the mix into a mug and pour 1 cup boiling water over it. Stir until the peanut butter chips have melted and the mixture is smooth. Serve immediately.

MAKES 1 QUART OF MIX TO YIELD 12 SERVINGS

The world changed when the Dutchman Coenraad van Houten invented a machine in the early nineteenth century that made it commercially viable to produce and sell cocoa powder.

Old-Fashioned Peppermint Stick Hot Chocolate Mix

Peppermint and chocolate together are hard to beat. Here is the perfect balance of chocolate's rich depth and creaminess with the spice and slight kick of peppermint.

1 cup sugar
1 cup natural cocoa powder
1 cup nonfat dry powdered milk
2 ounces bittersweet chocolate, chopped
½ cup crushed peppermint stick candy
2 teaspoons kosher salt
12 peppermint sticks for garnish (optional)

1. Combine the sugar, cocoa powder, powdered milk, chopped chocolate, peppermint candy, and salt in a large bowl. Pour into a 1-quart airtight container. If you wish to include the peppermint sticks with the mix, place them in a separate airtight container.

2. For a single serving, scoop ⅓ cup of the mix into a mug and pour 1 cup boiling water over it. Stir until the chocolate has melted and the mixture is smooth. Garnish with a peppermint stick, if desired, and serve immediately.

MAKES 1 QUART OF MIX TO YIELD 12 SERVINGS

The Carnation Company produced and sold the first hot chocolate mix in 1935. The company was also an innovator when it came to introducing single-serving envelopes and adding marshmallows to the mix.

Mocha Hot Chocolate Mix

I f you are fond of those coffee and chocolate combinations down at your local coffee bar, then I know you will like this mix. A good balance of the two flavors makes an excellent pick-me-up for the three o'clock blahs. And the price of this mix is easier to swallow.

1 cup sugar
1 cup natural cocoa powder
1 cup nonfat dry powdered milk
½ cup instant coffee or espresso powder
¾ cup miniature semisweet chocolate chips
2 teaspoons kosher salt

1. Combine the sugar, cocoa powder, powdered milk, instant coffee, chocolate chips, and salt in a large mixing bowl. Pour into a 1-quart airtight container.

2. For a single serving, scoop ⅓ cup of the mix into a mug and pour 1 cup boiling water over it. Stir until the chocolate chips have melted and the mixture is smooth. Serve immediately.

MAKES 1 QUART OF MIX TO YIELD 12 SERVINGS

Mexican Hot Cocoa and Chocolate Mix

Hot chocolate is serious business in Mexico. The Mexicans consume liquid chocolate almost as we do coffee. I think you will enjoy this mix for a great change of pace. Ibarra and Abuelita are both good Mexican chocolates and can be found in the Latin section of most grocery stores.

1 cup packed light brown sugar
1 cup natural cocoa powder
1 cup nonfat dry powdered milk
3 ounces Mexican chocolate, chopped
1 tablespoon ground cinnamon
2 teaspoons kosher salt
12 cinnamon sticks for garnish

1. Combine the brown sugar, cocoa powder, powdered milk, chopped chocolate, ground cinnamon, and salt in a large bowl. Pour into a 1-quart airtight container. Place the cinnamon sticks in a separate airtight container.

2. For a single serving, scoop ⅓ cup of the mix into a mug and pour 1 cup boiling water over it. Stir until the chocolate has melted and the mixture is smooth. Garnish with a cinnamon stick and serve immediately.

MAKES 1 QUART OF MIX TO YIELD 12 SERVINGS

Vanilla Hot Chocolate Mix

This mix is for all those folks who love white chocolate. The vanilla powder may be new to you, but many regular grocery stores now carry it, and most specialty food grocers do as well. You can do without it, but the vanilla powder does add an extra depth of flavor. The confectioners' or superfine sugar in this recipe will dissolve quickly and without any additional heat, which could cause the white chocolate chips to scorch.

1 cup confectioners' or superfine sugar
1 cup nonfat dry powdered milk
1 cup white chocolate chips
1 tablespoon vanilla powder
2 teaspoons kosher salt

1. Combine the sugar, powdered milk, chocolate chips, vanilla powder, and salt in a medium-size mixing bowl. Pour into a 1-quart airtight container.

2. For a single serving, scoop ⅓ cup of the mix into a mug and pour 1 cup boiling water over it. Stir until the chocolate has melted and the mixture is smooth. Serve immediately.

MAKES ABOUT 3 CUPS OF MIX TO YIELD 9 SERVINGS

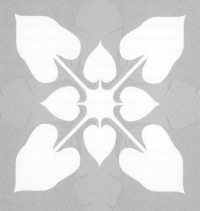

Super Classic Hot Cocoa and Chocolate Mix

A s in the Classic Hot Cocoa and Chocolate Mix (page 36), chocolate flavor abounds here. What distinguishes this mix is an added richness and mouth feel that comes from the powdered nondairy creamer. This recipe costs a bit more to make, but you may well think that it is worth the difference. You can also use whole powdered milk, which is available from baking stores and catalogs.

1 cup sugar
1 cup natural cocoa powder
½ cup nonfat dry powdered milk
½ cup vanilla-flavored nondairy powdered creamer (not low-fat)
½ cup miniature semisweet chocolate chips
2 teaspoons kosher salt
Miniature marshmallows for garnish

1. Combine the sugar, cocoa powder, powdered milk, powdered creamer, chocolate chips, and salt in a large bowl. Pour into a 1-quart airtight container. Place the marshmallows in a separate airtight container.

2. For a single serving, scoop ⅓ cup of the mix into a mug and pour 1 cup boiling water over it. Stir until the chocolate chips have melted and the mixture is smooth. Top with marshmallows and serve immediately.

MAKES 1 QUART OF MIX TO YIELD 12 SERVINGS

Super Mocha Hot Chocolate Mix

The combination of coffee and chocolate seems to be the flavor darling of those in my daughter's generation. Here is a mix that is super-rich and sure to satisfy their particular yen.

1 cup sugar
1 cup natural cocoa powder
1 cup nondairy powdered creamer (not low-fat)
½ cup instant coffee or espresso powder
¾ cup miniature semisweet chocolate chips
2 teaspoons kosher salt

1. Combine the sugar, cocoa powder, powdered creamer, instant coffee, chocolate chips, and salt in a large mixing bowl. Pour into a 1-quart airtight container.

2. For a single serving, scoop ⅓ cup of the mix into a mug and pour 1 cup boiling water over it. Stir until the chocolate chips have melted and the mixture is smooth. Serve immediately.

MAKES 1 QUART OF MIX TO YIELD 12 SERVINGS

Super Mexican Hot Cocoa and Chocolate Mix

This Mexican mix becomes more decadent with the addition of a little fat, in the form of powdered creamer. It is rounder and more complex than mixes made with nonfat dry powdered milk alone. As with the regular Mexican mix (see page 42), use Ibarra or Abuelita chocolate if possible.

1 cup packed light brown sugar
1 cup natural cocoa powder
½ cup nonfat dry powdered milk
½ cup cinnamon-flavored nondairy powdered creamer (not low-fat)
3 ounces Mexican chocolate, chopped
1 tablespoon ground cinnamon
2 teaspoons kosher salt
12 cinnamon sticks for garnish

1. Combine the brown sugar, cocoa powder, powdered milk, powdered creamer, chocolate, cinnamon, and salt in a large bowl. Pour into a 1-quart airtight container. Place the cinnamon sticks in a separate airtight container.

2. For a single serving, scoop ⅓ cup of the mix into a mug and pour 1 cup boiling water over it. Stir until the chocolate has melted and the mixture is smooth. Garnish with a cinnamon stick and serve immediately.

MAKES 1 QUART OF MIX TO YIELD 12 SERVINGS

According to an ancient Caribbean myth, it was the great Carib god Kobo Tano who gave humankind the gift of chocolate.

HOT CHOCOLATE WITH A TWIST

Let the serious fun begin. First we'll use some candy bars to create unique and interesting hot chocolate. Then we'll throw in a few other items, like ice cream, to make hot chocolate special. And in this chapter, hot chocolate also takes on guises from many different cultures. Hot tea and chocolate may sound strange, but the taste will convince you otherwise. What a great way to get the health benefits of both chocolate and tea! Can soy milk marry with chocolate for an amazing chocolate experience? Absolutely. Some recipes here may even return you to a childhood memory. Hot chocolates with a twist are fun to make and fabulous to drink.

Ghirardelli "Square" Caramel Hot Chocolate • Milk Chocolate Candy Bar Treat • Don Fry's Umbrian Fantasy Hot "Chocolate" • Jerry's Peanut Butter Dream • Darjeeling Tea Hot Chocolate • Chocolate Gravy • Summer's Frozen Hot Chocolate • Mystic Southeast Asian Hot Chocolate • Hot Chocolate à la Mode • Turkish-Style Mocha • Hot Cherry Chocolate • The Treehouse "Keep Your Heart Pumping" Hot Chocolate • Katrina's Guiltless Soy Milk Hot Cocoa • Raspberry Hot Chocolate • Chai Latte Hot Chocolate • Lavender Hot Chocolate • Hot Chocolate "Espresso" • Iced Hot Chocolate

Ghirardelli "Square" Caramel Hot Chocolate

Using caramel-filled chocolates is the easiest way to combine these flavors in a rich, decadent hot chocolate. There are several chocolate-and-caramel candies on the market, so if Ghirardelli chocolates aren't available in your neck of the woods, try Hershey's Kisses with caramel. But be sure to try this flavor combination.

2 cups half-and-half
One 6.9-ounce bag Ghirardelli milk chocolate squares with caramel filling
Whipped cream for garnish
Store-bought caramel sauce for garnish

1. Pour the half-and-half into a medium-size saucepan and warm over medium heat. Meanwhile, unwrap all of the chocolate squares and cut them into quarters.

2. When the half-and-half is just below a boil, with bubbles around the sides, whisk in the candy, and continue whisking until all the chocolate is melted and the mixture is smooth.

3. Serve immediately in cups with a dollop of whipped cream and a drizzle of caramel sauce.

SERVES 4 TO 6

A high-quality chocolate bar should be glossy and snap when you break it. It should also have a strong chocolate aroma and melt quickly on your tongue without ever having any waxiness or aftertaste.

Milk Chocolate Candy Bar Treat

Probably the simplest way to enjoy great hot chocolate is to melt your favorite candy bar with a little half-and-half. It's instant liquid candy. I suggest milk chocolate here, but don't let that limit you. Dark chocolate kisses, orange- or raspberry-flavored chocolate bars—the choices are all yours.

2 cups half-and-half
One 2- to 3-ounce milk chocolate bar, chopped
1 tablespoon natural cocoa powder
1 teaspoon arrowroot

1. Pour the half-and-half into a medium-size saucepan and place over medium heat until you begin to see bubbles around the edges.

2. Whisk in the chopped chocolate. Whisk in the cocoa powder and arrowroot. Let the mixture come to a boil, whisking constantly.

3. Let the mixture thicken slightly, then pour into mugs and serve immediately.

SERVES 4 TO 6

Don Fry's Umbrian Fantasy Hot "Chocolate"

Don Fry is a renowned writing coach from Charlottesville, Virginia, who eats Nutella by the spoonful, much to the dismay of his wife, Joan. On a trip to Umbria with the Frys, our group stopped at an Italian convenience store for gas and snacks. We sort of lost Don for a moment before spotting him in front of a display featuring five-gallon buckets of the hazelnut spread. There are no words to accurately describe the joy on that man's face as he pondered the many ways to consume that much Nutella. Don, here's a fantasy for you to enjoy.

2 cups half-and-half
⅔ cup packed Nutella, plus more for serving
2 teaspoons arrowroot

1. Heat the half-and-half in a medium-size saucepan over medium heat until you begin to see bubbles along the side.

2. Add the Nutella, whisking until smooth.

3. Whisk in the arrowroot. Let the mixture come to a boil. Remove from the heat.

4. Dollop a small amount of additional Nutella into 6 demitasse cups. Pour the hot mixture into the cups. If you have demitasse spoons, pass them for scooping out the Nutella in the bottom of each cup.

SERVES 6

Jerry's Peanut Butter Dream

My friend Jerry Ellis loves peanut butter and Ritz crackers. This treat calmed his hunger pains when he worked mountain outposts in three states for the Tennessee Valley Authority. A jar of peanut butter always goes on road trips and vacations, including trips to Spain to visit his granddaughter. A requirement for a happy marriage, according to Mr. Ellis, is making sure that there is always a jar of peanut butter in the house. For 50 years his wife, Tommie, has done just that. Here's a hot chocolate for them, and for all the other couples that have celebrated their fiftieth anniversary.

¼ cup semisweet chocolate chips
8 Ritz crackers
1 cup half-and-half
¼ cup sugar
½ cup creamy peanut butter
¼ cup whole milk or whole chocolate milk
4 scoops chocolate ice cream

1. Place the chocolate chips in a small bowl and heat in a microwave until melted. Dip a Ritz cracker halfway into the melted chocolate, allowing the excess to drip back into the bowl. Place on waxed paper to set. Repeat with the remaining crackers.

2. Heat the half-and-half and sugar in a medium-size saucepan over medium heat until just below a boil. The mixture will bubble around the edges. Stir in the peanut butter, whisking until smooth.

3. Remove from the heat and whisk in the milk. Place 1 scoop of ice cream into each of 4 mugs and top with the hot mixture. Let the ice cream melt slightly, then serve immediately, garnished with the Ritz crackers.

SERVES 4

Darjeeling Tea Hot Chocolate

This ultrasimple recipe has great flavor overtones. All you have to do is steep a bag of tea and add melted chocolate, but the result is far more complex and mysterious. Darjeeling is a light tea, but you can use a stronger black tea successfully as well.

4 ounces milk chocolate, chopped
1 black tea bag, such as Darjeeling
1 cup boiling water
Cream to taste
Sugar to taste

1. Place the chocolate in a small bowl and heat in a microwave until melted, being careful not to burn it.

2. In a large mug, steep the tea bag in the hot water for 5 minutes.

3. Stir in the melted chocolate. Add cream and sugar to taste and serve immediately.

SERVES 1

Chocolate Gravy

My barber, Sammy Giddens, loves food and restaurants, and we always have lively chats when I'm in his chair. When I told him about this book, he shared with me a tradition of his mother's family, who hail from Sampson County, North Carolina. Seems there was always a pot of hot chocolate simmering on the back of the stove, and about midmorning it was poured over toasted biscuits for a sweet pick-me-up. All this was new to me, and I told another foodie friend of mind, Sheri Castle, about the conversation. "Absolutely!" she exclaimed. "Do you want a recipe?" Before you go off thinking that this combination sounds crazy, make some biscuits (hey, the frozen ones work, too) and give it a try. I bet you'll be putting "choclick gravy" on a brunch buffet before long.

1 cup Dutch-processed cocoa powder
¾ cup sugar
½ cup all-purpose flour
2 cups whole milk
1½ teaspoons pure vanilla extract
6 leftover biscuits, lightly toasted

1. Whisk the cocoa powder, sugar, and flour together in a medium-size saucepan until well blended. Slowly whisk in the milk. Bring to a boil over medium-high heat, stirring constantly. Reduce the heat and simmer until slightly thickened, 3 to 5 minutes. Remove from the heat and stir in the vanilla extract.

2. Slightly crack the tops of the biscuits, place on serving plates, and pour the "gravy" over them. Serve at once.

SERVES 3 TO 6

Summer's Frozen Hot Chocolate

Probably one of the most famous drinks in New York City is the frozen hot chocolate at Serendipity 3. This celebrity haunt on East 60th Street features a wealth of ice cream inventions, but the frozen hot chocolate really packs them in, especially during the summer. I don't like standing in lines anywhere, so I decided to make frozen hot chocolate at home. Serendipity has published its "secret recipe," but you need a trip to Europe to purchase all the chocolates. Here's my version, which makes shopping easier.

1½ teaspoons sweetened cocoa powder
1½ teaspoons Dutch-processed cocoa powder
1½ tablespoons sugar
1 tablespoon salted butter, at room temperature
1½ cups whole milk
2 ounces bittersweet chocolate, chopped
2 ounces semisweet chocolate, chopped
2 ounces milk chocolate, chopped
4 cups crushed ice
Sweetened whipped cream for garnish
Grated chocolate of your choice for garnish

1. Place a double boiler over medium heat. Add both cocoa powders, the sugar, and the butter. Whisk until the cocoas and sugar have melted and creamed together with the butter.

2. Add a little of the milk. Add the chocolates, whisking as they melt. Slowly pour in additional milk, reserving 1 cup milk for step 3. Whisk until the mixture is smooth. Remove from the heat and let cool to room temperature.

3. In a blender, make 3 servings at a time. Add ½ cup of the chocolate base, ½ cup milk, and about 2 cups crushed ice. Blend until smooth, adding more ice or liquid as needed to reach a perfect texture. (Repeat with remaining ingredients or store any unused chocolate base in the refrigerator, covered.) Pour frozen hot chocolate into large goblets and top with whipped cream and grated chocolate. Serve immediately with a straw and a long spoon.

SERVES 6

Mystic Southeast Asian Hot Chocolate

A lemongrass infusion gives this chocolate drink a mysterious, faraway note. If you enjoy a touch of heat, add some chili paste while whipping the cream to top the hot chocolate.

2 cups half-and-half
One 3-inch piece fresh lemongrass or 3 sticks dried lemongrass
1 teaspoon orange zest
4 ounces semisweet chocolate, chopped
¼ teaspoon curry powder
Whipped cream for garnish (optional)

1. Place a medium-size saucepan over medium heat and add the half-and-half, lemongrass, and orange zest. Bring to a boil, taking care not to let boil over. Reduce the heat to a simmer and cook for 10 minutes, covered.

2. Remove the lemongrass and whisk in the chocolate until melted. Divide the mixture between 2 mugs and sprinkle ⅛ teaspoon curry powder over each. Serve immediately, with whipped cream if desired.

SERVES 2

Hot Chocolate
à la Mode

Belinda Ellis, a food scientist, product developer, and fellow southern foodways preservationist, showed up one day at the "hot chocolate lab" (my kitchen) with a grocery bag full of ice cream, declaring, "You laughed at me when I suggested ice cream in hot chocolate, so I'm here to prove that the two are made to go together, winter or summer." She's a pretty demanding woman, not to be messed with when on a mission. Ten minutes later, I was a convert. A scoop of ice cream in a simple hot chocolate is a thing of beauty.

1 cup whole milk
½ cup semisweet chocolate chips
1 scoop coffee or vanilla ice cream

1. Pour the milk into a large glass measuring cup. Heat for 2 to 3 minutes in the microwave, until hot. Add the chocolate chips and let sit for 1 minute. Then whisk until all the chocolate has completely melted.

2. Place 1 large scoop of ice cream into a large mug. Pour the hot chocolate over the ice cream and serve immediately with a long spoon.

SERVES 1

Turkish–Style Mocha

Cardamom is a spice that creeps into taste memory without being immediately recognized. Strong coffee, chocolate, and cardamom combine here to create an enticing flavor that you won't soon forget.

¾ cup ground dark roast coffee
1 tablespoon ground cardamom
6 cups water
2 cups whole milk or half-and-half
½ cup sugar
½ cup chocolate syrup

1. Combine the coffee and cardamom in a coffee filter. Brew the coffee in a coffeemaker with the water.

2. Meanwhile, heat the milk, sugar, and chocolate syrup in a medium-size saucepan over medium heat. Stir in the brewed coffee, pour into 4 cups, and serve immediately.

SERVES 4

Hot Cherry Chocolate

I loved chocolate-covered cherries as a kid. Heck, I still like them today. This hot chocolate brings back memories in a smooth and soothing way.

6 cups whole milk
2 cups heavy cream
1½ cups chocolate syrup
½ cup plus 2 tablespoons maraschino cherry syrup
1 tablespoon confectioners' sugar
4 red maraschino cherries with stems

1. Combine the milk, 1 cup of the cream, the chocolate syrup, and ½ cup of the cherry syrup in a medium-size saucepan over medium heat. Cook, stirring, until the mixture has bubbles around the edge of the saucepan. Do not let the mixture boil. Keep warm over low heat while you whip the cream.

2. Using an electric mixer, beat the remaining 1 cup cream until foamy. Gradually add the confectioners' sugar and the remaining 2 tablespoons of cherry syrup, beating until soft peaks form.

3. Pour the hot chocolate into 4 mugs. Spoon the whipped cream over each serving of chocolate and top with a cherry. Serve immediately.

SERVES 4

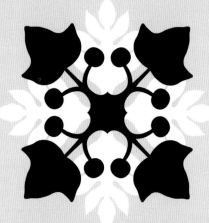

The Treehouse "Keep Your Heart Pumping" Hot Chocolate

My mentor, Toni Allegra, e-mailed me from her office in the trees overlooking Napa Valley to tell me about how cinnamon was supposed to help lower cholesterol. Her sister, Nikki Lastreto, had discovered that a half teaspoon of cinnamon a day would do the trick. Toni and her husband, Donn, have been taking this "medication" with another heart-healthy substance—chocolate. I threw in the soy milk to make a trinity of virtuous flavors. Remember, the darker the chocolate, the greater the advantages. If only all remedies could be so tasty!

1 cup vanilla-flavored soy milk
2 ounces dark chocolate (at least 70 percent cacao), chopped
2 teaspoons sugar (optional)
1 teaspoon ground cinnamon

1. Pour the soy milk into a medium-size saucepan and place over medium heat. Bring to just under a boil; look for small bubbles on the sides of the pan. Remove from the heat. Whisk in the chocolate until melted and smooth. Return to the heat and whisk in the sugar, if desired, and the cinnamon. Simmer, whisking, for another minute.

2. Pour the hot chocolate into 2 cups and serve immediately.

SERVES 2

Katrina's Guiltless Soy Milk Hot Cocoa

The budding actress and theatrical buff Katrina Moore decided to be a vegetarian after she left for college. I challenged her to develop a hot chocolate that was perfect for her dietary needs, and she surprised me with a hot chocolate that everyone can love. It's a wonderful guiltless indulgence to enjoy.

2 cups soy milk
2 tablespoons natural cocoa powder
1 teaspoon pure vanilla extract
Honey to taste

1. Pour the soy milk into a medium-size saucepan and place over medium-high heat. Bring to just under a boil; look for small bubbles on the sides of the pan. Reduce the heat and whisk in the cocoa powder. Let simmer for 2 to 3 minutes.

2. Remove from the heat and whisk in the vanilla extract. Pour the hot cocoa into 2 mugs and add honey to taste.

SERVES 2

The first cocoa beans to land on American shores came from the Dutch in the 1600s and were sent to New Amsterdam, which is now known as New York City.

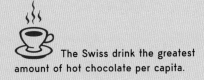

Raspberry Hot Chocolate

Raspberry and chocolate join together to become a taste delight for any and all. You can transform this recipe into one for strawberry hot chocolate if you prefer by simply substituting strawberry syrup for the raspberry. This recipe is also a base for real Swiss-style *schoggi,* the Swiss version of hot chocolate.

3½ ounces bittersweet chocolate, chopped
3¼ cups whole milk
2 tablespoons sugar
1 large egg yolk
½ cup raspberry syrup, or more to your taste

1. Combine the chocolate and ¼ cup of the milk in a small heavy saucepan over medium-low heat. Gradually heat, stirring, until the chocolate has melted and the mixture is smooth. Remove from heat and set aside.

2. In a large saucepan over medium-high heat, bring the remaining 3 cups milk to just under a boil; look for small bubbles on the sides of the pan. Remove from the heat and add ½ cup of the milk to the chocolate mixture, stirring until well blended.

3. In a measuring cup, beat the sugar and egg yolk together with a fork. Add the egg mixture to the chocolate mixture and stir until smooth. Pour this mixture into the remaining milk in the large saucepan. Place the pan over medium heat and cook for about 3 minutes, stirring constantly. Do not boil. Remove from the heat and stir in the raspberry syrup.

4. Pour the hot chocolate into 4 mugs and serve immediately.

SERVES 4

Chai Latte
Hot Chocolate

Chai has really moved into the mainstream over the past few years, and with good reason—it's refreshing and different. Adding chocolate seems natural, and I think the result is one of the best beverages in the book. Use one of the premixed chai concentrates sold in cartons, such as Tazo.

½ cup chai mix concentrate
½ cup half-and-half
2 ounces semisweet chocolate, chopped
2 marshmallows for garnish (optional)

1. Pour the chai mix and half-and-half into a medium-size saucepan and place over medium heat. Bring to just under a boil; look for small bubbles on the sides of the pan. You will smell the spices in the chai. Remove from the heat and whisk in the chocolate until it has melted and the mixture is smooth.

2. Pour the hot chocolate into 2 cups. Serve immediately, with a marshmallow on top if desired.

SERVES 2

Lavender Hot Chocolate

Lavender is surprising in its affinity to chocolate. It greatly enriches the intensity of the chocolate, and the aroma will delight your senses. This recipe makes the best hot chocolate for a relaxing moment after a long, hard, cold day. Most health-food stores and gourmet stores carry lavender buds, sometimes already ground.

> 4 cups whole milk or half-and-half
> 1 tablespoon pulverized dried lavender buds
> 1 ounce bittersweet chocolate, chopped
> ¼ cup Dutch-processed cocoa powder
> 3 tablespoons sugar
> ⅛ teaspoon kosher salt
> ½ teaspoon pure vanilla extract

1. Pour the milk into a medium-size saucepan and add the lavender. Place over medium heat and bring just to a boil. Remove from the heat and allow to steep for 5 to 8 minutes, or longer for a stronger lavender flavor.

2. Return the saucepan to the heat. Whisk in the chocolate until melted and smooth. Whisk in the cocoa powder, sugar, and salt. Remove from the heat and whisk in the vanilla extract.

3. Divide among 4 Irish coffee glasses, straining out the lavender if desired. Serve immediately.

SERVES 4

The L. A. Burdick chocolate company's cafés, in Walpole, New Hampshire, and Cambridge and Northampton, Massachusetts, offer unparalleled chocolate drinks accompanied by fabulous handmade chocolates and other treats.

Hot Chocolate "Espresso"

Deep, dark, and potent, this hot chocolate is just like great espresso but with a wickedly chocolate taste explosion. Like espresso, serve it in demitasse cups.

½ cup heavy cream
½ cup whole milk
3 ounces bittersweet chocolate (at least 70 percent cacao), chopped

1. Bring the cream and milk to a simmer in a small heavy saucepan over medium-high heat. Remove from the heat and quickly add the chocolate, stirring until melted and very smooth. Return to medium-low heat and warm until a bubble or two form on the surface, about 3 minutes.

2. Pour the hot chocolate into 4 demitasse cups and serve immediately.

SERVES 4

The Hotel Morgana in Rome serves one of the most decadent and dark hot chocolates I've ever tasted with its European breakfast.

Iced Hot Chocolate

This hot chocolate is from the pastry chef Nicole Plue at Julia's Kitchen, the restaurant at the food and art museum Copia, in the Napa Valley. She uses 72 percent Guittard chocolate, which I recommend. Copia serves this drink as a sweet, small finish at the end of the meal, in a frosty little shot glass.

3 cups half-and-half
1½ cups whole milk
⅓ cup plus 1 tablespoon firmly packed dark brown sugar
Pinch of salt
3 whole star anise (optional)
7 ounces bittersweet chocolate, chopped

1. In a medium-size saucepan over medium heat, combine the half-and-half, milk, brown sugar, salt, and the star anise, if desired. Bring to a boil, stirring occasionally. Remove from the heat and set aside for 20 minutes.

2. Meanwhile, place the chocolate in a large heatproof bowl and melt it in the microwave, being careful not to burn it.

3. Slowly add the hot liquid to the melted chocolate, about ½ cup at a time. Mix thoroughly to combine. Strain the mixture through a fine-mesh sieve to remove the star anise, if using.

4. Chill the mixture for at least 4 hours and up to overnight. Serve straight up.

SERVES 6 TO 8

Taste a piece of 62 percent cacao chocolate. It has a distinct cherry flavor overtone.

H O T
CHOCOLATE
WITH SPIRIT

Hot chocolate becomes an adult treat in this chapter. Already a sensuous and seductive beverage, hot chocolate undergoes a transformation with the use of some carefully selected brandies and liqueurs. There's a hot chocolate in this chapter for all occasions. Some are for two to share. Others are for a house full of family and friends. Remember, though, that most of these recipes can be made without the alcohol and thus served to the kids and teetotalers. Experiment with your favorite liqueurs, because it's impossible to list all the great combinations here.

Chocolate to the Fifth Power • Hot Chocolate with Citrus, Cinnamon, and Brandy • Lovers' Hot Chocolate • Brandied Hot Chocolate • Hot Chocolate Nog • Christmas Eve Hot Chocolate • A Chill Chaser • Chestnut Hot Chocolate • Vanilla Hot Chocolate Seduction • Mint Julep Hot Chocolate • "Let It Snow" Cocoa

Chocolate to the Fifth Power

Chocolate, chocolate, chocolate, chocolate, and more chocolate: this adult hot chocolate will fill you with soothing tastes and relaxing feelings. It is a chocoholic's perfect after-dinner drink. You might want to cut the recipe in half and share it with someone very special. If you want to make Chocolate to the Sixth Power, top it with a dollop of the chocolate whipped cream from page 22.

    2 cups whole chocolate milk
    Four 1.55-ounce milk chocolate bars, broken into chunks
    2 tablespoons natural cocoa powder
    2 teaspoons arrowroot
    4 tablespoons crème de cacao
    4 tablespoons Godiva chocolate liqueur
    Marshmallows for garnish

1. Pour the chocolate milk into a medium-size saucepan and place over medium heat. Bring to just under a boil; look for small bubbles on the sides of the pan.

2. Whisk in the chocolate until smooth. Whisk the cocoa powder into the mixture until smooth, then whisk in the arrowroot. Stir in the crème de cacao and Godiva liqueur.

3. Pour into 4 mugs and serve immediately with marshmallows on top.

SERVES 4

Melted chocolate should never feel hot when you touch it to your lip, but just warm. Keeping the chocolate from overheating will prevent it from scorching and tasting bitter.

Hot Chocolate with Citrus, Cinnamon, and Brandy

This recipe is adapted from the New York City restaurant Eleven Madison Park. It is great for a gathering of friends on a blustery winter's night or for a holiday party. The citrus and cinnamon add freshness and vibrancy, and the chocolate and brandy give this drink its creamy richness.

6 cups half-and-half
One 4-inch cinnamon stick
Zest of 1 orange
½ cup firmly packed light brown sugar
9 ounces bittersweet chocolate, chopped
½ cup brandy

1. In a large saucepan, combine the half-and-half, cinnamon stick, orange zest, and brown sugar. Place over medium heat and bring to a simmer, stirring constantly. Bring to just under a boil; look for small bubbles on the sides of the pan. Turn off the heat and keep pan warm.

2. In a large double boiler over low heat, melt the chocolate, and then strain the half-and-half mixture into it through a fine-mesh sieve. Whisk constantly until the mixture is smooth. Remove from the heat and stir in the brandy. Pour the hot chocolate into 8 mugs and serve immediately.

SERVES 8

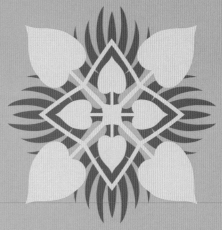

Lovers' Hot Chocolate

Amaretto is the Italian liqueur of love, and it blends beautifully with chocolate and coffee, both of which are in this drink, an offering to the senses. Use a richly flavored chocolate ice cream here.

1 ounce crème de cacao
1 ounce amaretto
1½ cups hot brewed coffee
4 tablespoons chocolate ice cream
8 pecan halves, chopped, for garnish

Divide the crème de cacao, amaretto, and coffee between 2 Irish coffee glasses, stirring to blend. Top each with 2 tablespoons of the ice cream and half of the chopped pecans. Serve immediately.

SERVES 2

Brandied Hot Chocolate

Brandy is one of life's true pleasures, along with chocolate, of course. The two mingle extremely well, making this hot chocolate perfect for after dinner with friends and good conversation.

2 teaspoons cornstarch
1½ cups whole milk
½ cup water
10 ounces bittersweet chocolate (less than 60 percent cacao), chopped
⅛ teaspoon kosher salt
½ cup heavy cream
1 tablespoon natural cocoa powder
2 tablespoons brandy

1. Make a slurry by whisking together the cornstarch and 2 tablespoons of the milk in a small bowl.

2. Pour the water into a large saucepan and place over high heat. Bring the water to a boil, reduce the heat to low, and add the chocolate and salt. Whisk until smooth.

3. Add the cream and the remaining milk to the pan. Slightly increase the heat and cook, stirring, until the mixture is very smooth and heated through. Whisk in the cocoa powder.

4. Whisk the cornstarch mixture again, then add to the chocolate mixture in the saucepan. Cook, whisking, until slightly thickened, 2 to 3 minutes. Stir in the brandy and simmer 1 minute. Pour the hot chocolate into 8 mugs and serve immediately.

SERVES 8

Hot Chocolate Nog

For a fun twist on a festive beverage, add some chocolate to your eggnog. This recipe is another wonderful hot chocolate for a crowd, with the eggnog and chocolate blending for the best of holiday traditions. You could leave out the bourbon before serving the kids, but most of the merrymakers will want the "nog."

1 quart store-bought eggnog
2 cups whole milk
½ cup chocolate syrup
1 cup bourbon
¼ teaspoon ground nutmeg, plus more for garnish

1. Pour the eggnog, milk, and chocolate syrup into a medium-size saucepan and place over medium heat. Stir constantly and bring to just under a boil; look for small bubbles on the sides of the pan. Remove from the heat and stir in the bourbon and nutmeg.

2. Ladle the hot chocolate into 8 mugs. Sprinkle additional nutmeg on top for garnish and serve hot.

SERVES 8

Christmas Eve Hot Chocolate

The house is full of family and friends and everybody is stir-crazy. So . . . whip up a batch of this hot chocolate. There's a jolt for those who need it, and some wonderful mellow flavors for those who want to take the edge off. Have one of the mixes from the Hot Chocolate Mixes and Super Mixes chapter (see pages 35–47) on hand for the kids, and everyone is covered.

1½ cups dark roast hot brewed coffee
8 ounces bittersweet chocolate, chopped
¼ cup sugar
3 ounces Kahlúa
3 ounces crème de cacao
2 ounces brandy
¼ cup heavy cream
Whipped cream or marshmallows for garnish

1. Place the brewed coffee, chocolate, and sugar in a medium-size saucepan over medium-low heat. Cook, stirring, until the chocolate has melted and the sugar has dissolved. Do not boil. Remove from the heat and stir in the Kahlúa, crème de cacao, brandy, and heavy cream.

2. Pour into cups and serve immediately, topped with whipped cream or marshmallows.

SERVES 8 IN REGULAR CUPS OR 16 IN ESPRESSO CUPS

 Chocolate "mellows" over time, like wine.

A Chill Chaser

A better name for this recipe might be "The Most Romantic of Hot Chocolates." Two liqueurs and some dark rum transform simple hot chocolate into a sophisticated beverage. It is also one that you might want to share by the fireplace. You may use your favorite hot chocolate here, but the Classic Hot Cocoa and Chocolate Mix (page 36) is excellent.

2 ounces Irish cream liqueur, such as Baileys
2 ounces dark rum
1 ounce crème de cacao
2 cups of your favorite hot chocolate
Whipped cream for garnish

1. Divide the Irish cream liqueur, rum, and crème de cacao between 2 Irish coffee glasses. Pour 1 cup hot chocolate into each glass and stir.

2. Top with a dollop of whipped cream and serve immediately.

SERVES 2

Chestnut Hot Chocolate

Because I grew up in the South, chestnuts never made a big impression on me, and quite frankly they were difficult to find. That has changed now in most areas, at least when it comes to chestnut puree. I fell in love with the chestnut-chocolate combination years ago when I prepared a chestnut-chocolate pâté dessert from *Bon Appétit* magazine. This is that dessert in a mug.

3 cups whole milk
½ cup sugar
⅛ teaspoon ground cinnamon
⅛ teaspoon kosher salt
12 ounces dark chocolate, chopped into small pieces
12 ounces chestnut puree
½ cup Frangelico
½ cup brandy
Whipped cream or marshmallows for garnish

1. Pour the milk, sugar, cinnamon, and salt into a large saucepan. Place over medium-high heat and cook, stirring, until the mixture is hot, about 5 minutes.

2. Add the chocolate and stir until it has completely melted. Add the chestnut puree. Cook, stirring constantly, until the puree is totally incorporated. Stir in the Frangelico and brandy.

3. Pour the hot chocolate into 8 mugs and top with whipped cream or a marshmallow. Serve immediately.

SERVES 8

Vanilla Hot Chocolate Seduction

Vanilla hot chocolate has a mysterious pull, especially with the addition of some white chocolate liqueur. With the orange tones of the Triple Sec, this hot chocolate really is seductive.

1½ cups whole milk or half-and-half
½ cup vanilla syrup
⅛ teaspoon kosher salt
1 vanilla bean
6 ounces white chocolate, chopped
2 ounces white chocolate liqueur
2 ounces Triple Sec
Marshmallows for garnish
Cocoa powder for garnish

1. Pour the milk, vanilla syrup, and salt into a medium-size saucepan. Place over medium heat and cook, stirring, until the mixture is hot. Do not boil.

2. Split the vanilla bean lengthwise and scrape out the seeds. Add the seeds to the saucepan.

3. Add the white chocolate and stir until the chocolate has melted and the mixture is smooth. Don't rush this step by turning up the heat, or the white chocolate may seize. Stir in the liqueurs and blend.

4. Pour the hot chocolate into 4 mugs and serve immediately, topped with marshmallows and a sprinkle of cocoa powder.

SERVES 4

Mint Julep Hot Chocolate

You can keep the horserace, but I'll take the julep, with chocolate added, that is. Now you have a winner. Add a bit of bourbon to a dessert or beverage and you have one of my favorite things.

2 cups half-and-half
12 miniature peppermint patties, chopped
2 tablespoons arrowroot
¼ cup bourbon, or more to your taste
Fresh mint sprigs for garnish

1. Heat the half-and-half in a medium-size saucepan over medium heat until you begin to see bubbles around the edges. Reduce the heat, add the peppermint patties, and whisk until melted and smooth.

2. Whisk in the arrowroot and allow the mixture to cook and thicken for a few minutes. Remove from the heat and stir in the bourbon. Pour the mixture into mugs and garnish with mint sprigs. Serve immediately.

SERVES 4 TO 6

"Let It Snow" Cocoa

Gather skiers, snowboarders, and sled drivers to partake of this warming hot chocolate. You can mix up this recipe, put it in a slow cooker, and let folks serve themselves. Or fill thermos jugs for those who want to head back out into the snow. One caveat about the slow cooker: don't use the lid, as it will cause condensation to drip back into the hot chocolate, diluting it. As a serving option, you can put the whiskey beside the slow cooker and let guests pour their own as they ladle out the hot chocolate.

10 cups whole milk
1 cup heavy cream or half-and-half
1 cup sugar
⅛ teaspoon kosher salt
1 cup natural cocoa powder
1½ cups whiskey, or to taste
Sweetened whipped cream for garnish (optional)

1. In a large pot, combine the milk, cream, sugar, and salt. Place over medium heat, whisking occasionally, until hot but not boiling. Whisk in the cocoa powder until no lumps remain. Bring to just under a boil; look for small bubbles around the sides of the pan. Remove from the heat and stir in the whiskey.

2. Pour the cocoa into 12 mugs and serve immediately, topped with whipped cream if desired; or pour all the cocoa into a slow cooker and let guests serve themselves.

SERVES 12

Measurement Equivalents

Liquid Conversions

U.S.	Metric
1 tsp	5 ml
1 tbs	15 ml
2 tbs	30 ml
3 tbs	45 ml
¼ cup	60 ml
⅓ cup	75 ml
⅓ cup + 1 tbs	90 ml
⅓ cup + 2 tbs	100 ml
½ cup	120 ml
⅔ cup	150 ml
¾ cup	180 ml
¾ cup + 2 tbs	200 ml
1 cup	240 ml
1 cup + 2 tbs	275 ml
1¼ cups	300 ml
1⅓ cups	325 ml
1½ cups	350 ml
1⅔ cups	375 ml
1¾ cups	400 ml
1¾ cups + 2 tbs	450 ml
2 cups (1 pint)	475 ml
2½ cups	600 ml
3 cups	720 ml
4 cups (1 quart)	945 ml
(1,000 ml is 1 liter)	

Weight Conversions

U.S./U.K.	Metric
½ oz	14 g
1 oz	28 g
1½ oz	43 g
2 oz	57 g
2½ oz	71 g
3 oz	85 g
3½ oz	100 g
4 oz	113 g
5 oz	142 g
6 oz	170 g
7 oz	200 g
8 oz	227 g
9 oz	255 g
10 oz	284 g
11 oz	312 g
12 oz	340 g
13 oz	368 g
14 oz	400 g
15 oz	425 g
1 lb	454 g

Oven Temperature Conversions

°F	Gas Mark	°C
250	½	120
275	1	140
300	2	150
325	3	165
350	4	180
375	5	190
400	6	200
425	7	220
450	8	230
475	9	240
500	10	260
550	Broil	290

Please note that all conversions are approximate.

Index

H

About the Author

Fred Thompson is a food writer, a food stylist, and a culinary developer. He is the author of *Lemonade*, *Iced Tea*, *Crazy for Crab*, and *The Big Book of Fish & Shellfish* and is a columnist for the *News & Observer* in Raleigh, North Carolina. He also writes for *Fine Cooking* magazine, *Wine & Spirits*, and *Every Day with Rachael Ray*, and is a popular cooking school teacher. He lives in Raleigh and New York City.